D1307341

WEATHERWISE

VAPOR, RAIN, and SNOW

The Science of CLOUDS and PRECIPITATION

Paul Fleisher

LERNER PUBLICATIONS COMPANY · MINNEAPOLIS

Lerner Publications Company
A division of Lerner Publishing Group, Inc.
241 First Avenue North
Minneapolis, MN 55401 U.S.A.

Website address: www.lernerbooks.com

Library of Congress Cataloging-in-Publication Data

Fleisher, Paul.
    Vapor, rain, and snow : the science of clouds and
precipitation / by Paul Fleisher.
        p.   cm. — (Weatherwise)
    Includes bibliographical references and index.
    ISBN 978–0–8225–7534–4 (lib. bdg. : alk. paper)
    1. Clouds—Juvenile literature. 2. Precipitation
(Meteorology)—Juvenile literature. I. Title.
  QC921.35.F555 2011
  551.57′6—dc22   2009041720

Manufactured in the United States of America
1 – PC – 7/15/10

CONTENTS

| INTRODUCTION |

Weather is what happens in the air around us. But a lot of weather is really about water. When we think about weather, we think about rain or snow. We think about clouds and humidity. Each of those involves a form of water.

Air is a mixture of clear, colorless gases. Water vapor is one of those gases. (It is the gas form of water.) The amount of water vapor in the air is always changing. On humid days, the air contains a lot of water vapor. When the air is dry, it holds very little water vapor.

Water typically falls from the sky in the form of rain or snow. It eventually returns to the sky when it turns into water vapor.

Meteorology is the science of weather. For meteorologists to understand weather, they have to know what happens to water in the air. They have to be able to measure the amount of water in the air. They have to recognize different kinds of clouds and the weather these clouds bring with them. They have to know about different types of precipitation, such as mist, rain, sleet, and snow. And they have to know how water vapor carries the sun's energy from one part of the atmosphere to another.

CHAPTER ONE

WATER IN THE AIR

Earth has only a limited amount of water. That water is recycled again and again. Water vapor in the air comes from oceans, from the land, and even from the leaves of plants. Water falls back to the ground as rain or snow. Plants take in some of the water. A small amount is frozen into glaciers. Some water flows to streams, lakes, and rivers. It eventually flows back to the oceans, where it may become vapor again. This process is called the water cycle.

Water moves through the water cycle in three different states. Ice is solid water. So are frost and snow. Rain and dew are liquid water. Tiny droplets of liquid water make up clouds. Water vapor is an invisible gas.

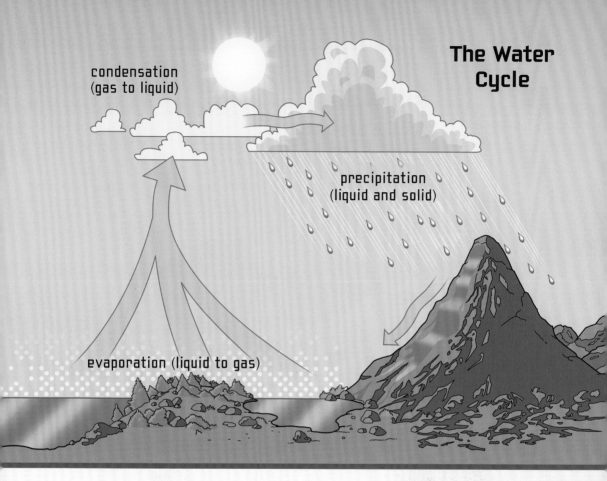

The Water Cycle

condensation (gas to liquid)

precipitation (liquid and solid)

evaporation (liquid to gas)

Water takes all three forms in the atmosphere, the layer of air that surrounds Earth.

Water changes back and forth between states. When water changes from a liquid to a solid, it freezes. When ice changes from solid to liquid, it melts. When water changes from liquid to gas, it evaporates. And it condenses when it changes from gas to liquid.

FASCINATING FACT:

How much water is in the atmosphere at any one time? Enough to cover the whole Earth with water about 1 inch (2.5 centimeters) deep.

Water evaporates from the surface of a calm lake. In the cooler air above the lake, the water condenses into fog.

A lot of energy is needed for water to change from solid to liquid. Water needs even more energy to change from liquid to gas. That energy comes from the sun. Evaporating water carries the sun's energy with it in the form of heat. Whatever area water evaporates from gets cooler. When water evaporates from our skin, we no longer feel as hot. When water condenses, it releases its energy. The air around it gets warmer. This energy helps clouds form. It fuels powerful storms. As a result, evaporation and condensation transfer huge amounts of energy into the atmosphere.

SUBLIMATION AND DEPOSITION

Sometimes water changes directly from a solid to a gas. On cold, dry days, snow slowly disappears without melting. The snow changes into vapor in the air. It never becomes liquid. The name for this process is sublimation. Sublimation happens in your refrigerator too. When we leave an ice cube tray in the freezer for a long time, the ice cubes shrink. They haven't melted. They have sublimated. Sublimation happens most easily when the air is dry. Water molecules on the surface of the ice or snow take energy from their surroundings— enough energy to change into a gas.

The opposite process also happens. When it's cold, water vapor can freeze directly to a surface. Ice crystals form without ever becoming liquid water. This process is called deposition. On a warm, humid day, take a package of frozen food out of the freezer. In a few minutes, frost forms on the outside. The crystals are deposited from the water vapor in the air. Deposition is common in cold clouds. Tiny ice crystals form without ever becoming water droplets. Like condensation, deposition also releases energy.

WATER VAPOR FROM THE AIR NEARBY HAS FROZEN ON THESE LEAVES, FORMING ICE CRYSTALS.

MOISTURE IN THE AIR

Humidity is the amount of water vapor in the air. Warm air holds much more water vapor than cool air. But at any temperature, there's a limit to how much water vapor the air can hold. When the air is at that limit, we say it is saturated. It doesn't take much water vapor for cold air to be saturated. At 32°F (0°C), saturated air only holds 0.03 percent water vapor. Warm air holds much more vapor. On a hot, humid day, water vapor can be as much as 4 percent of the air. We feel uncomfortable on days like that. Moisture from our skin can't evaporate to cool us off.

Humidity is tricky to measure. It's not very helpful to only know how much water vapor is in the air. We have to compare that with how much vapor the air could hold at that temperature. This measurement is called relative humidity. Scientists must know the temperature to measure relative humidity. Relative humidity is measured as a percent. Relative humidity of 100 percent means the air is completely saturated—it is holding all the water vapor it possibly can.

Relative humidity changes hour by hour. Without the sun's heat, the air cools during the night. It warms up throughout the day. In the morning, the air is still cool. Remember, cool

A HYGROMETER MEASURES THE AMOUNT OF WATER VAPOR IN THE AIR. IT ALSO MEASURES AIR TEMPERATURE. TOGETHER, THE TWO MEASUREMENTS GIVE THE RELATIVE HUMIDITY.

air can't hold very much water vapor. So the relative humidity might be fairly high. Later in the day, as temperatures rise, the air could hold more water vapor. The relative humidity gets lower because the temperature has changed.

Another measurement of humidity is the dew point. The dew point is the temperature at which the air would become saturated. The more moisture in the air, the higher the dew point. On humid summer days, dew points may be 70°F (21°C) or higher. In the winter, dew points are much lower.

The dew point helps meteorologists predict the lowest overnight temperature. The temperature begins to decrease after the sun sets. But as the air nears the dew point, water vapor condenses. Water changing from a gas to a liquid releases heat energy. That extra heat keeps the air from getting any colder.

MEASURING HUMIDITY

Meteorologists use tools called hygrometers to measure relative humidity. One kind of hygrometer has two thermometers side by side. The bulb of one thermometer is covered with a wet, hanging piece of cloth called a wick. This thermometer is called the wet bulb. The other thermometer has no wick. It's the dry bulb. Evaporation from the cloth cools the wet bulb. That lowers its temperature. The dry bulb measures the actual air temperature.

THE HAIR HYGROMETER

Human hair absorbs water. It gets longer when the humidity is high. This process makes straight hair go limp. Curly hair gets frizzy.

A hair hygrometer consists of a few strands of hair stretched between two posts. Their length changes with the humidity. Levers connect the posts to a pointer. The pointer moves as the hair stretches or shrinks. It shows the humidity on a dial.

Meteorologists measure relative humidity by comparing the difference in temperature between the thermometers. When the air is dry, lots of water evaporates from the wet bulb. That cools the thermometer, so it shows a lower temperature than the dry bulb. What if the air is saturated? Then no water evaporates from the wick. Both thermometers give the same reading. The relative humidity measures 100 percent.

Some hygrometers measure humidity electrically. When the air is more humid, it conducts, or carries, electricity better. A meter in the hygrometer measures how much electricity can flow between two wires. That measurement reveals how much moisture is in the air.

HUMIDITY AND COMFORT

Humidity can affect how we feel. In winter the air gets very dry. Moisture evaporates from our skin. Lips get chapped. Hands get rough and dry.

A humidifier is a machine that adds water to the air. Many people humidify their homes during winter months. Less water evaporates from the skin, and we feel warmer.

When it's hot, we perspire. The sweat evaporates. That process cools the skin. But when the air is very humid, sweat doesn't evaporate quickly. It's hard to stay comfortable. The body's temperature rises. In extreme cases, this situation can be dangerous. It can cause heat exhaustion or heat stroke.

PLAYING SPORTS CAN CAUSE US TO SWEAT. SWEAT ON THE SKIN HELPS COOL THE BODY. BE SURE TO DRINK PLENTY OF WATER ON HOT, HUMID DAYS.

In the summer, people use dehumidifiers to take water from the air. More moisture evaporates from our skin, and we feel cooler. Air conditioners cool the air, but they also take moisture out of the air. That makes us feel more comfortable. Fans also help us feel cool. Moving air evaporates more water than still air. Moving air carries away water vapor, so more water on our bodies can evaporate.

AN EXPERIMENT: EVAPORATION AND COMFORT

You can feel the difference that evaporation makes. You'll need a plastic sandwich bag, some tape, and a bowl of water at room temperature.

Put one hand inside the bag. Gently tape it around your wrist. Leave the other hand open to the air. Wait a few minutes. The hand in the bag will become wet with sweat. Dip your other hand in the bowl of water. Both hands are damp. Both are the same temperature. Compare how they feel.

The hand inside the bag probably feels uncomfortable. The bag keeps the sweat from evaporating. Air can't carry the moisture away from your skin. The water on your other hand can evaporate. That hand feels more comfortable.

CHAPTER TWO

CLOUDS

What is a cloud? A cloud is made of billions of tiny droplets of water. That's all it is. The droplets are so small and light that they just hang in the air. Clouds might look heavy and solid, but they're not.

Have you ever wondered what a cloud feels like? If you've ever walked through fog, you already know. Fog is just a cloud at ground level.

HOW DO CLOUDS FORM?

Clouds form when moist air rises. When air rises, it cools. The cool air becomes saturated. Water vapor condenses on tiny particles in the air. The water forms droplets. These droplets create clouds. As more water vapor condenses, the clouds get thicker.

Air can rise to form clouds in four ways. **OROGRAPHIC LIFTING.** Winds push air over an obstacle such as a mountain range or an island. The air rises to pass over the obstacle. This motion is called orographic lifting. As the air rises, it gets cooler.

CLOUDS FORM BY OROGRAPHIC LIFTING IN SOUTH AFRICA. AIR COOLS WHILE RISING OVER TABLE MOUNTAIN.

Clouds form as water vapor condenses in the cool air.

WEATHER FRONTS. A mass of cold air sometimes pushes under warmer air. This movement is called a cold front. The dense cold air lifts the warm air above it. The warm air cools, and clouds form.

Cold Front

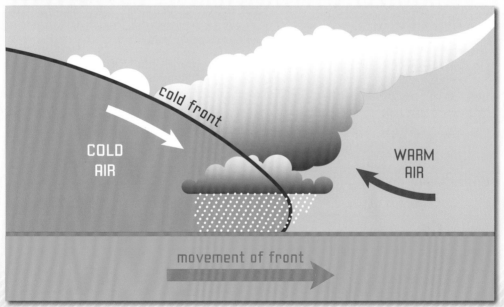

cold front

COLD AIR

WARM AIR

movement of front

Warm Front

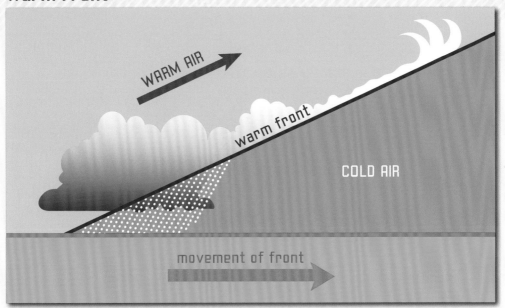

Sometimes warm air slides over cooler air. This movement is called a warm front. Again, the warm air rises. When it does, its water vapor condenses into clouds.

CONVERGENCE. Two air masses sometimes converge. That means they come together. Some of the air is pushed upward. As it rises, it also cools. Again, clouds form.

CONVECTION. Air near Earth's surface is heated by the sun. The warm air floats upward. Meteorologists call the rising airflow a convection current. Rising currents of warm air are called thermals. Water vapor in the thermals condenses as it cools. This process usually produces puffy cumulus clouds.

Water vapor has to condense onto something. The air is full of tiny particles called aerosols. Some are bits of sand or soil. Others are specks of salt from ocean spray. Some come from volcanoes or fires. Others come from factory smoke or car exhaust.

Aerosols are so small we can't see them. But they're big enough for water vapor to condense on them. What looks like an empty glass of air actually holds thousands of these tiny particles.

Each particle acts as a center around which water vapor can condense. Clouds start forming when the relative humidity is about 75 percent. As the humidity increases, more water vapor condenses. The clouds get bigger and thicker.

TYPES OF CLOUDS

Meteorologists divide clouds into four main groups—high clouds, middle clouds, low clouds, and clouds with vertical growth. Each group includes several kinds of clouds. You can often see more than one kind of cloud in the sky at a time.

THIN, WISPY CIRRUS CLOUDS APPEAR IN A BRIGHT BLUE SKY.

HIGH CLOUDS. High clouds form at 20,000 feet (6,096 meters) or higher. At that height, the air is very cold. So high clouds are usually made of ice crystals. There is not much moisture this high in the air. So high clouds are thin. All high clouds look white. They don't bring rain or snow.

Cirrus clouds are thin, wispy high clouds. They form feathery streamers. Cirrus clouds usually appear in fair weather. If more cirrus clouds form, a warm front may be coming. That means rain may arrive in a day or two.

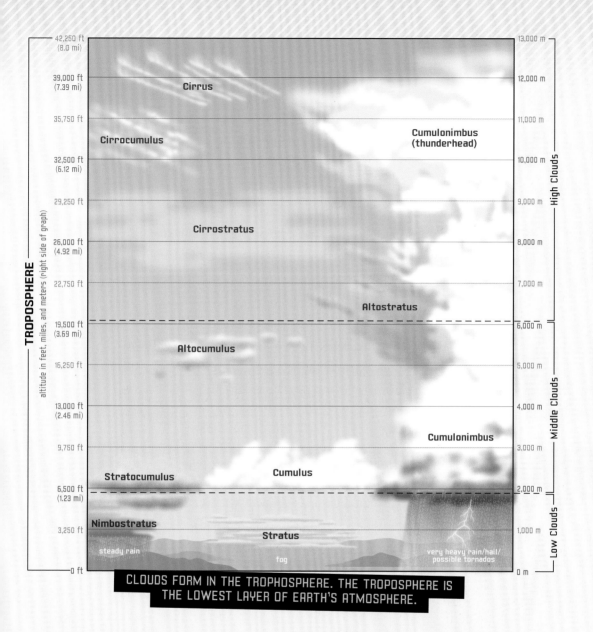

TROPOSPHERE

altitude in feet, miles, and meters (right side of graph)

42,250 ft (8.0 mi) — 13,000 m
39,000 ft (7.39 mi) — 12,000 m
35,750 ft — 11,000 m
32,500 ft (6.12 mi) — 10,000 m
29,250 ft — 9,000 m
26,000 ft (4.92 mi) — 8,000 m
22,750 ft — 7,000 m
19,500 ft (3.69 mi) — 6,000 m
15,250 ft — 5,000 m
13,000 ft (2.46 mi) — 4,000 m
9,750 ft — 3,000 m
6,500 ft (1.23 mi) — 2,000 m
3,250 ft — 1,000 m
0 ft — 0 m

High Clouds
Middle Clouds
Low Clouds

Cirrus

Cirrocumulus

Cumulonimbus (thunderhead)

Cirrostratus

Altostratus

Altocumulus

Cumulonimbus

Stratocumulus

Cumulus

Nimbostratus

Stratus

steady rain

fog

very heavy rain/hail/ possible tornados

CLOUDS FORM IN THE TROPHOSPHERE. THE TROPOSPHERE IS THE LOWEST LAYER OF EARTH'S ATMOSPHERE.

Cirrocumulus clouds are small, high, puffy clouds. They often form rippled rows. A sky filled with cirrocumulus clouds is sometimes called a mackerel sky. The rows of clouds look like the markings on the side of a fish. Cirrostratus clouds form a thin, white haze across the sky.

MIDDLE CLOUDS. Middle clouds form from 6,500 feet (1,981 m) to 20,000 feet (about 6,096 m) in the air. They are usually a mixture of water droplets and ice crystals.

Altostratus clouds are flat and gray middle clouds. They cover the sky like a thin sheet. A dim, hazy sun shows through them, making a bright spot in the sky. These clouds usually mean a steady rain is on the way.

Altocumulus clouds are puffy middle clouds. They're shaded gray. They often form rows or waves across the sky. In warm weather, altocumulus clouds mean thunderstorms may come later in the day.

Altostratus and altocumulus clouds cover a darkening sky. The wavy part of the cloud formation is the altocumulus clouds. The flatter clouds are altostratus clouds.

LOW CLOUDS. Low clouds usually form below 6,500 feet (1,981 m). They are made of liquid water droplets.

Low clouds called stratus clouds make a gray, flat sheet that covers the whole sky. Stratus clouds might bring mist or drizzle, but they usually don't bring rain. Fog is a stratus cloud at ground level.

Stratocumulus clouds are large and gray. They have dark, flat bases. Stratocumulus clouds may appear in rows. We often see patches of sky in between these clouds.

Nimbostratus clouds are low rain clouds. They are dark gray. Nimbostratus clouds are thicker than stratus clouds. They bring steady rain.

THESE THREE PHOTOS SHOW DIFFERENT EXAMPLES OF LOW CLOUDS *(FROM TOP TO BOTTOM):* STRATUS CLOUDS, STRATOCUMULUS CLOUDS, AND NIMBOSTRATUS CLOUDS.

These puffy cumulus clouds look like bales of cotton against the blue sky.

CLOUDS WITH VERTICAL GROWTH. Some clouds climb upward as they form. This growth happens as warm thermals rise through cooler air on a sunny day.

As thermals rise, they cool. Water vapor condenses. It forms white cumulus clouds. Cumulus clouds look like cotton balls floating in a blue sky. They have a flat base. Cumulus clouds float as low as 3,300 feet (1,005 m) above the ground.

Cumulus clouds are fair-weather clouds. But on hot, humid days, they grow larger. The clouds keep rising higher and higher. They can then develop into storm clouds.

Cumulonimbus clouds are also called thunderheads. They tower above the ground. The bottoms of these clouds get very dark. Their tops can rise as many as 10 miles (16 kilometers) high.

The clouds flatten out on top, forming an anvil shape. The tops of the clouds are made of ice crystals.

Cumulonimbus clouds create powerful storms. They bring heavy rain and strong winds. They produce lightning and thunder. Sometimes they form hail. Tornadoes may even form in their violent winds.

THE ANVIL SHAPE OF THIS CUMULONIMBUS CLOUD COULD MEAN THAT A THUNDERSTORM IS ON THE WAY.

MAKE YOUR OWN CLOUDS

When we see our breath on a cold day, we're seeing a little cloud. The air in our lungs is warm and moist. We exhale into the cold air. The water vapor in our breath condenses. It forms a cloud.

When we boil water in a kettle, we also make a cloud. Hot water vapor comes out the spout. It meets the cooler air. The vapor condenses into a cloud of tiny water droplets.

UNUSUAL CLOUDS

Some clouds form in surprising ways. Other clouds can take unusual shapes. Oddly shaped clouds sometimes form above a mountain. They are called lenticular clouds. They are shaped like lenses. The wind pushes them into a flat, rounded shape. People sometimes think they are flying saucers or other unidentified flying objects (UFOs).

High-flying jets can leave long streaks of clouds behind them. These clouds are called contrails. The word is a shortening of "condensation trails." Jet exhaust contains millions of tiny particles for water vapor to condense around. On dry days, contrails evaporate quickly. If there's enough moisture in the air, contrails may spread, covering a wide path in the sky.

Lenticular clouds form above a mountain range in Norway. The morning sunrise colors the clouds above them a rosy pink.

A JET LEAVES BEHIND A PAIR OF CONTRAILS AS IT CROSSES THE SKY.

Much of what we think is light-colored smoke coming out of smokestacks is really water vapor. In cold air, it condenses to form white clouds. Yellowish or brownish clouds are often called smog. Smog is a form of air pollution. Smog is a combination of smoke and fog. Factories and car exhaust put chemicals in the air. The chemicals mix with water vapor.

Smog can damage people's lungs. The National Weather Service, a U.S. government agency, warns people when smog levels are expected to be especially harmful.

PREDICTING THE WEATHER WITH CLOUDS

Clouds tell a lot about what weather we can expect. For example, small cumulus clouds usually signal fair weather. So do a few cirrus clouds. When the contrails of jets evaporate quickly, it means the air is dry. Don't expect rain anytime soon.

Cumulus clouds sometimes continue to grow larger and higher. When this happens, thunderstorms may develop later in the day.

Cirrostratus clouds tell us a weather front is coming. So do altostratus clouds. If these clouds begin to thicken, rain or snow may follow.

CHAPTER THREE

PRECIPITATION

Water that falls from the sky is called precipitation. Precipitation forms in clouds. When the air is dry, precipitation is unlikely. But if there is enough water vapor, clouds thicken. Rain, snow, sleet, or hail begins to fall.

Meteorologists think rain usually forms in one of two ways. The most common way is the Bergeron process. It is named for meteorologist Tor Bergeron, who helped explain it. This process involves cold clouds. Water usually freezes at 32°F (0°C). But in cold clouds, water droplets stay liquid even at much lower temperatures. The water is supercooled.

Heavy water droplets fall during a thunderstorm. Thunder clouds build high into the atmosphere, where the air is much cooler.

In a cold cloud, ice crystals also form around tiny particles. Water evaporates from the cloud droplets and then freezes onto nearby ice crystals. The crystals gather more water from the droplets and get heavier. Finally, they get heavy enough to fall through the cloud.

If the lower air is warmer, the crystals melt on the way down. They become rain. If the air below is cold, the precipitation falls as snow or sleet.

Meteorologists think the other way rain forms is through collision and capture. This process takes place in warm clouds. At first, cloud droplets are much too light to fall as rain. They float in the air.

The droplets bump into one another. They join together and become heavier. The larger drops begin to fall through the cloud. They bump into other droplets. More droplets add to the size of each drop. The drops grow heavier and fall faster. As they fall, they create air currents. These tiny breezes pull more cloud droplets into the falling drops.

The drops fall to the ground as rain. How many cloud droplets does it take to make an average raindrop? About a million!

When precipitation falls from a cloud, it doesn't always reach the ground. The air below the cloud may be very dry. Raindrops and snowflakes sometimes evaporate as they fall. But when the air below the cloud gets humid enough, the rain or snow begins to fall again.

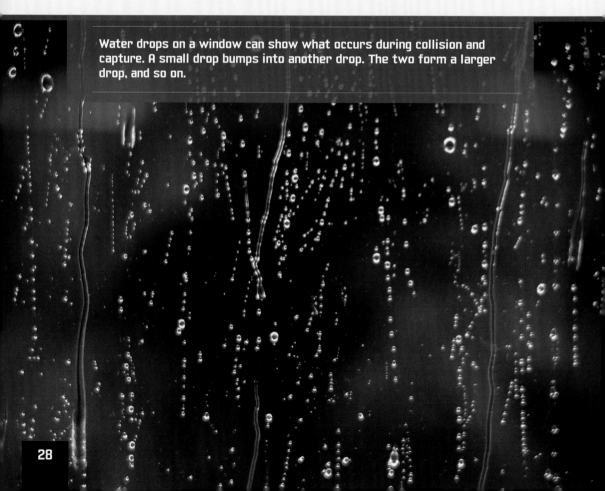

Water drops on a window can show what occurs during collision and capture. A small drop bumps into another drop. The two form a larger drop, and so on.

TYPES OF PRECIPITATION

Precipitation happens in all seasons. It happens at many different temperatures. So precipitation takes many different forms.

Some peopple imagine a teardrop shape when they think of raindrops falling. But raindrops are actually round. Water molecules pull together into the smallest possible shape—a sphere, or ball. Large drops flatten out as they fall. That's because the air underneath pushes against them.

Raindrops don't get larger than about 0.2 inches (0.5 cm) across. Anything larger breaks apart into smaller drops.

Drizzle is made of very small raindrops, less than 0.02 inches (0.5 millimeters) across. Drizzle usually falls from stratus clouds. Drizzle drifts down slowly. Not much water reaches the ground when it is drizzling.

AS A WATER DROPLET FALLS FROM A LEAF, IT TAKES THE ROUND SHAPE OF A RAINDROP.

Mist is made of droplets that are even lighter and tinier than drizzle. Mist drifts in the air. It hardly falls at all. Mist usually comes with stratus clouds or fog.

Sometimes rain falls from a cloud but evaporates before it reaches the ground. This rain forms gray streaks, called virga, beneath the clouds. We see these streaks of rain falling, but the ground stays dry.

Sleet is frozen rain. It is made of tiny pellets of ice. Sleet forms when raindrops fall through a cold layer of air and freeze on their way down. Sometimes the raindrops start out as snowflakes. They melt while falling through warmer air. Then they refreeze into sleet.

A sleet storm is noisy. Sleet bounces when it hits the ground. The ice pellets rattle against the trees. They tap on the roofs and windows of houses.

Glaze is also called freezing rain. It is different from sleet. Glaze falls as liquid water. But the water is supercooled. The temperature at ground level is below freezing too. When the rain hits the surface, it freezes. It forms a coating of ice on trees and cars. It freezes on roads and electrical wires.

People often call this an ice storm. An ice storm can be beautiful. But freezing rain causes a lot of damage. Cars skid on icy roads. Trees bend or break under the weight of the ice. Power lines come crashing down.

A process called deposition forms snow crystals. Water vapor is deposited as ice on bits of airborne dust. If the air contains enough moisture, the crystals grow. Snow crystals start out tiny. But as more ice is deposited on the crystals, they get heavier. They bump into one another and freeze together. When they are heavy enough, the crystals fall as snow.

FREEZING RAIN COATS THESE ROADS AND TREE BRANCHES WITH A SLIPPERY LAYER OF GLAZE.

Snow crystals always have six sides. A flat crystal with six branches is called a dendrite. This is the shape we usually think of as a snowflake. But not all snow crystals are shaped this way. Some snow crystals are shaped like needles. Others are six-sided plates. Some are shaped like rods. The shape depends on how cold it is and on the amount of moisture in the air.

If the air is very cold, snowfall is light and powdery. If the temperature is near the freezing point, snow clumps together. It forms larger flakes. The snow is wet and heavy.

CAN TWO SNOWFLAKES LOOK ALIKE?

Is it true that no two snowflakes are exactly alike? Not likely. Trillions of snowflakes fall to Earth each year. So many snowflakes probably do look alike. But no one has time to compare them all.

HAILSTONES FORM WHEN FROZEN RAINDROPS ARE HELD IN THE SKY BY STRONG STORM WINDS.

Hail is ice, but we're most likely to see it falling during warm months. Hail forms in thunderstorms. Powerful winds carry raindrops high into the thundercloud. The air there is very cold. The raindrops freeze. Strong storm winds hold the frozen drops up for a long time. The small ice pellets fall through the cloud, collecting a coating of more ice as they go. Upward winds blow the frozen balls back up toward the top of the cloud. They may travel up and down through the cloud many times. Each time, they gather another layer of ice.

The hailstones grow heavier. Finally, the wind can't hold them up anymore. They fall to the ground. Most hailstones are no bigger than peas. But sometimes they can grow bigger than golf balls. Hailstorms can destroy crops and damage cars and buildings.

FASCINATING FACT:

The largest hailstone ever found in the United States fell in Aurora, Nebraska, in 2003. It was 7 inches (17.8 cm) across, with a circumference (distance around) of 18.75 inches (47.6 cm). That's bigger than a grapefruit.

Rime formed on the outer edges of these leaves. When water vapor came in contact with the cold leaves, it froze into ice crystals.

Rime is made of ice crystals. It looks like frost. However, frost forms on clear, cold mornings. Rime forms in a fog or mist. Water droplets touch a cold surface and freeze to it. Rime makes a feathery coating on cold surfaces.

Graupel is another kind of frozen precipitation. It forms when snowflakes gather extra frozen cloud droplets. Graupel takes the shape of rounded, icy clumps. A common name for graupel is snow pellets.

NOT QUITE PRECIPITATION

Dew and frost also seem to be types of precipitation. But they don't actually fall from the sky. Both dew and frost form at ground level. And they only form when skies are clear. So they're not really precipitation.

DEW DROPLETS SPARKLE AT THE ENDS OF BLADES OF GRASS.

On a cool, clear morning, the grass and leaves may be wet with dew. At night, air near the ground gets cool. It can't hold as much moisture anymore, so water vapor condenses on low objects. It forms droplets of dew. In desert regions, where there is little rain, some plants and animals depend on dew for much of their water.

Dew doesn't form when the wind is blowing. The moving air evaporates any water that condenses. Dew doesn't form on cloudy nights either. The clouds act like a blanket. They keep the ground from cooling enough to form dew.

Frost is very much like dew. On cold, clear nights, frost forms on surfaces near the ground. The air at ground level gets colder than the freezing point of water. Water vapor is deposited on surfaces as ice crystals.

Like dew, frost doesn't form on cloudy or windy nights. Wind mixes warmer air from above with the cold air at ground level. Farmers in Florida often put large fans in their orange groves. When it gets cold, the fans keep frost from harming their crop.

RAINMAKERS

People need water to drink. Crops need rain to grow. So people have tried many ways to make rain fall. Many cultures have rainmaking ceremonies. But it's not easy to affect the weather.

Scientists have also tried to create rain. The most successful method is called cloud seeding. Airplanes scatter tiny chemical particles in cold clouds *(right).* Ice crystals grow on the particles. They later fall as rain or snow. This method can work, but only if clouds are already in the sky.

MEASURING PRECIPITATION

Meteorologists measure precipitation with rain gauges. A rain gauge gives the level of precipitation in inches or centimeters. Rainfall is usually measured over a twenty-four-hour period.

Most rain gauges have a wide funnel for collecting rainwater. The funnel empties into a long tube marked with measurements along the side.

The mouth of the funnel is ten times the width of the tube. This design makes it easier to measure small amounts of rain. The funnel gathers ten times as much rain as the tube alone would. Scientists then divide the amount of water in the collecting tube by ten to figure out how much rain actually fell.

Some rain gauges measure automatically. They have pairs of small measuring cups. Each cup measures 0.01 inch (0.25 mm) of rain. The cup tips when it is full. When one cup tips, the other starts to fill. A switch counts the number of times the cups tip over.

Sometimes we only get a tiny amount of rain. Anything less than 0.01 inch (0.25 mm) of rain is called a trace.

Measuring snowfall is trickier. Wind piles up the snow in some places. In other places, wind blows away snow. Meteorologists use a stick to measure snow in an open area. They push the stick down through the snow and read the depth. They measure in several different places. Then they take an average of their readings.

FASCINATING FACT:

The driest place on Earth is Chile's Atacama Desert. It gets less than 0.5 inches (1.3 cm) of rain a year. During many years, no rain falls there at all.

Meteorologists are not sure about the world's wettest place. One possibility is Mount Wai'ale'ale on the Hawaiian island of Kauai. It gets more than 40 feet (12 m) of rain per year!

Some snow is light and fluffy. It might take 10 inches (25.4 cm) of fluffy snow to equal 1 inch (2.5 cm) of rain. Other snowfalls are wet and heavy. About 4 inches (10.2 cm) of wet snow could equal an inch of rain. The only way to measure the amount of water in the snow is to melt it and pour the water into a rain gauge.

WHAT IS ACID RAIN?

Acid rain is rainwater mixed with dangerous chemicals. Air is sometimes polluted with sulfur dioxide or nitrogen oxide. These chemicals come from factory smoke, car exhaust, and volcanic eruptions. They mix with the rain. They form sulfuric acid and nitric acid. These acids can burn other materials or dissolve them away.

Acid rain harms plants and animals. It also damages buildings. Some factories have cleaning devices on their smokestacks. These "scrubbers" remove much of the pollutants. Fewer chemicals rise into the air, which helps reduce acid rain.

CHAPTER FOUR

RAINBOWS, HALOS, AND SUN DOGS

Sunlight is made of many different colors of light. A triangular glass prism can bend rays of light. The prism lets us see all these colors. Drops of water can also act like tiny prisms.

Sometimes the sun shines on raindrops in the sky. The drops break the light into many colors. They form a rainbow. The inner surface of a raindrop acts like a mirror. The raindrops reflect the light back to our eyes. That's how we see a rainbow.

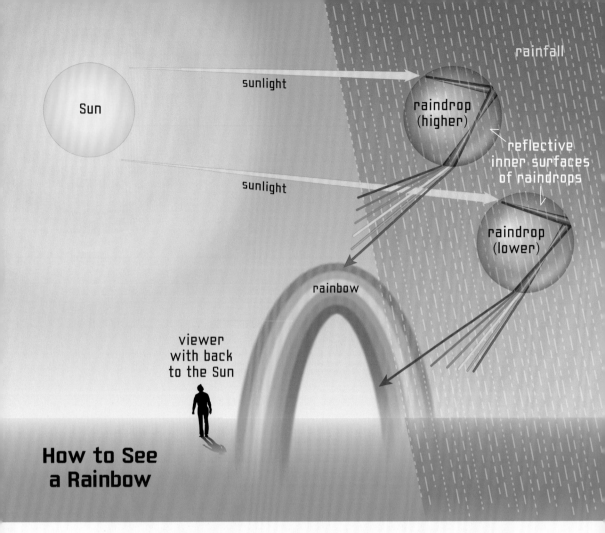

Sun

sunlight

sunlight

rainfall

raindrop
(higher)

reflective
inner surfaces
of raindrops

raindrop
(lower)

rainbow

viewer
with back
to the Sun

How to See
a Rainbow

To see a rainbow, it must be raining. And the sun must be shining at the same time. A rainbow always appears in the opposite direction from the sun. A person must turn his or her back to the sun to see a rainbow.

Ice crystals can act like prisms too. Thin cirrostratus clouds are made of ice crystals. When they cover the sky, we may see a ring of light around the sun or the moon. It's called a halo. The crystals bend the sunlight so we see a circle. A halo often means rain or snow is coming.

MAKE YOUR OWN RAINBOW

To make a rainbow, you'll need a garden hose and a sunny day. Set the nozzle of the hose to make a fine spray. Stand so the sun is behind you. Spray the water into the air at about eye level. You should see a rainbow.

Adjust the nozzle to make larger or smaller drops. Change the angle of your spray. See how these changes affect the appearance of the rainbow.

When the sun is lower in the sky, we may see patches of light on either side of the sun. They usually appear in pairs. These patches are called sun dogs. Sun dogs also appear when there are cirrostratus clouds in the sky. They usually have faint rainbow colors.

Sun dogs get their name because they seem to tag along with the sun like puppies. The scientific name for these bright spots is parhelia. Like halos, sun dogs may mean that precipitation is on the way.

SUN DOGS APPEAR AROUND THE SUN ON AN ISLAND IN CANADA'S HUDSON BAY.

METEOROLOGY IN THE TWENTY-FIRST CENTURY

Meteorologists have learned a lot about clouds and rain in the past century. In 1900 we could watch clouds only from the ground. The invention of the airplane allowed us to get a closer look. In modern times, scientists can use satellites to observe couds. Satellites are machines people launch into space. They circle Earth, taking photos and making measurements. They can study the clouds from above.

Satellites send back pictures of clouds taken from high above Earth. The thickest clouds are most likely to have rain or snow. Satellites also take pictures with infrared light. We can't see infrared light. But water vapor absorbs it. Infrared pictures show the moisture in the air. These images are helpful in predicting storms.

This satellite view of Earth shows cloud formations above the oceans and continents.

A METEOROLOGIST AT THE NATIONAL HURRICANE CENTER IN MIAMI, FLORIDA, TRACKS A HURRICANE USING COMPUTERS AND SATELLITE PICTURES. INFORMATION FROM SATELLITE PICTURES AND FROM RADAR EQUIPMENT HELPS RESEARCHERS MONITOR EARTH'S WEATHER.

Meteorologists also track precipitation with radar. Radar is a system that sends out beams of radio waves, another kind of light we cannot see. The radio waves bounce off falling rain or snow. They travel back to the radar station. Radar can even tell scientists how heavy the precipitation is.

Modern science has taught us much about clouds and precipitation. But there is still more to find out. Can we learn to make rain more effectively? Are there ways to make storms less violent? Can we make better weather forecasts? Improving our knowledge about clouds and precipitation will help us answer those questions.

GLOSSARY

aerosol: a tiny particle that floats in the air

air mass: a large body of air that extends for hundreds or thousands of miles (kilometers) horizontally and keeps a pretty constant temperature and humidity level as it travels

Bergeron process: the process by which rain forms in cold clouds

collision and capture: the process by which rain forms in warm clouds

condensation: the process by which a gas (such as water vapor) changes to a liquid (such as water)

convection: the movement of heat through liquids and gases

convergence: a weather condition in which winds push air toward a region of the atmosphere

deposition: the process by which a gas (such as water vapor) changes directly to a solid (such as ice)

dew point: a measure of humidity; the temperature at which air would become saturated and water would condense

evaporation: the process by which a liquid (such as water) changes to a gas (such as water vapor)

front: a boundary zone between two air masses that differ in temperature and humidity

humidity: the amount of water vapor in the air

hygrometer: a device that measures relative humidity

meteorology: the science of weather

molecule: the smallest part of a substance that contains all chemical properties of the substance

orographic lifting: air rising as the wind pushes it over mountains. This upward movement cools the air and may form clouds.

parhelia: bright spots that appear around the sun, also called sun dogs

precipitation: any form of moisture that falls from the sky, such as rain, snow, or sleet

prism: a piece of clear glass or crystal that breaks white light into its many colors

relative humidity: the measure of how much water vapor the air can hold at a certain temperature

satellite: a machine that orbits (circles) Earth

saturation: at any given temperature, the condition in which the air holds as much water vapor as it can

sublimation: the process by which a solid (such as ice) changes directly into a gas (such as water vapor)

troposphere: the lowest level of the atmosphere, up to about 6.6 miles (11 km) above Earth's surface, where all weather takes place

supercooled water: water that remains liquid even though it is colder than the freezing point (32°F, or 0°C)

water cycle: the never-ending process by which water evaporates from Earth's surface and then condenses to return to the surface again as precipitation

water vapor: water in its gas form

SELECTED BIBLIOGRAPHY

Aguardo, Edward, and James E. Burt. *Understanding Weather and Climate*. 3rd ed. Upper Saddle River, NJ: Pearson Education, 2004.

Ahrens, C. Donald. *Meteorology Today*. 8th ed. Belmont, CA: Brooks/Cole, 2007.

Allaby, Michael. *The Facts on File Weather and Climate Handbook*. New York: Facts on File, 2002.

Lutgens, Frederick, and Edward J. Tarbuck. *The Atmosphere: An Introduction to Meteorology*. 10th ed. Upper Saddle River, NJ: Prentice Hall, 2007.

Mayes, Julian. *Understanding Weather: A Visual Approach*. London: Arnold, 2004.

Nese, Jon M., et al. *A World of Weather: Fundamentals of Meteorology*. Dubuque, IA: Kendall/Hunt Publishing, 1996.

Reynolds, Ross. *Firefly Guide to Weather*. Buffalo: Firefly Books, 2005.

FOR FURTHER READING

Fleisher, Paul. *Doppler Radar, Satellites, and Computer Models: The Science of Weather Forecasting*. Minneapolis: Lerner Publications Company, 2011. Meteorology is a complex, imperfect science. This book in the Weatherwise series explores how meteorologists predict coming weather patterns, gather data, and track storms.

———. *Gases, Pressure, and Wind: The Science of the Atmosphere*. Minneapolis: Lerner Publications Company, 2011. What makes the wind blow? This book in the Weatherwise series explains how energy from the sun and the gases around Earth work together to create Earth's weather patterns.

———. *Lightning, Hurricanes, and Blizzards: The Science of Storms*. Minneapolis: Lerner Publications Company, 2011. What causes thunderstorms and lightning? Where do hurricanes form? This book in the Weatherwise series discusses how and where Earth's storms occur.

Fridell, Ron. *Protecting Earth's Water Supply.* Minneapolis: Lerner Publications Company, 2009. Explore the causes of problems facing Earth's water supply, and discover new trends, new technology, and new solutions.

Hannah, Julie, and Joan Holub. *The Man Who Named the Clouds.* Morton Grove, IL: Albert Whitman and Company, 2006. Luke Howard was an amateur meteorologist who invented the system we use to identify clouds. This book tells the story of Howard's early life and teaches readers how to keep a weather journal.

Johnson, Rebecca L. *Satellites.* Minneapolis: Lerner Publications Company, 2006. Find out more about how meteorologists and other scientists use satellites, as well as how they solve problems and develop new technology.

Locker, Thomas. *Water Dance.* San Diego: Voyager Books, 2002. This book captures the different stages of the water cycle in bold landscape and seascape paintings.

Staub, Frank. *The Kids' Book of Clouds and Sky.* New York: Sterling, 2003. A fun question-and-answer format helps readers learn more about clouds, air pollution, humidity, and other weather topics.

WEBSITES

California Institute of Technology: A Guide to Snowflakes
http://www.its.caltech.edu/~atomic/snowcrystals/class/class.htm
Visit this site for close-up photos and detailed descriptions of the many different types of snowflakes.

Environmental Protection Agency: Thirstin's Water Cycle
www.epa.gov/ogwdw/kids/flash/flash_watercycle.html
This animated web page explains each stage of the water cycle in a fun, interactive way.

National Oceanographic and Atmospheric Administration, U.S. Dept. of Commerce
http://www.noaa.gov
The official website of the U.S. National Oceanographic and Atmospheric Administration features the latest weather and climate news.

National Weather Service
http://www.nws.noaa.gov
Check out the National Weather Service's site for local and national weather warnings and forecasts.

University of California, San Diego: Water Cycle Animated Diagram
http://earthguide.ucsd.edu/earthguide/diagrams/watercycle
This site features an interactive diagram that illustrates how water moves through the water cycle and the different forms it can take.

University Corporation for Atmospheric Research: Web Weather for Kids
http://eo.ucar.edu/webweather
Visit this site for weather-related games, stories, safety tips, and cool do-it-yourself activities.

INDEX

ABOUT THE AUTHOR

Paul Fleisher is a veteran educator and the author of dozens of science titles for children, including the Secrets of the Universe series, the Early Bird Food Web series, and *The Big Bang* and *Evolution* for the Great Ideas of Science series. He is also the author of *Parasites: Latching On to a Free Lunch.* He lives with his wife in Richmond, Virginia.

PHOTO ACKNOWLEDGMENTS

The images in this book are used with the permission of: © Mandel Ngan/AFP/Getty Images, p. 1; © Photodisc/Getty Images, pp. 3, 4, 22; © Ryan McVay/Lifesize/Getty Images, p. 5; © Victor Zastol`skiy/Dreamstime.com, p. 6; © Bill Hauser/Independent Picture Service, p. 7; © Nicolas "Kipourax" Paquet/Flickr/Getty Images, p. 8; © Adam Hart-Davis/ Photo Researchers, Inc., p. 9; © GIPhotoStock/Photo Researchers, Inc., p. 10; © Phil Date/ Shutterstock Images, p. 12; © Katja Zimmermann/Taxi/Getty Images, p. 13; © Eric Isselée/ Dreamstime.com, p. 14; © Janis Jansons/Dreamstime.com, p. 15; © Mohamed Shahid/ Dreamstime.com, p. 16 (top); © Laura Westlund/Independent Picture Service, pp. 16 (bottom), 17, 19, 40; © Johnny Lye/Dreamstime.com, p. 18; © Mark Schneider/Visuals Unlimited, Inc., pp. 20, 21 (middle); © Marli Miller/Visuals Unlimited, Inc., p. 21 (top); © Glenn Oliver/Visuals Unlimited, Inc., p. 21 (bottom); © Robert Harding Picture Library/SuperStock, p. 23 (top); © David R. Frazier Photolibrary, Inc./Alamy, p. 23 (bottom); © larigan-Patricia Hamilton/Flickr/Getty Images, p. 24; © Constantin Opris/Dreamstime.com, p. 25; © Juliane Jacobs/Dreamstime.com, p. 26; © Thomas Wiewandt/Visuals Unlimited, Inc., p. 27; © Wolfgang Ante/Flickr/Getty Images, p. 28; © Petra Wegner/Alamy, p. 29; © Tim Holt/ Photo Researchers, Inc., p. 30; © Larry W. Smith/Getty Images, p. 31; © Richard Walters/ Visuals Unlimited, Inc., p. 32 (inset); © Stan Honda/AFP/Getty Images, p. 32 (background); © Perennou Nuridsany/Photo Researchers, Inc., p. 33; © Ernie Janes/Alamy, p. 34; © Wenbin Yu/Dreamstime.com, p. 35; © Inga Spence/Visuals Unlimited, Inc., p. 36; © Martin Green/ Dreamstime.com, p. 37; © Christopher Pillitz/The Image Bank/Getty Images, p. 38; © Mylightscapes/Dreamstime.com, p. 39; © Sue Flood/Stone/Getty Images, p. 41; © Stocktrek Images/Getty Images, p. 42; © Joe Raedle/Getty Images, p. 43.

Front cover: © ideeone/iStockphoto.com.